For Tom and Freya with all my love, with special thanks to Leo and Humphrey for good advice and most of all to Noah for the inspiration

First published 2017 by Walker Books Ltd,
87 Vauxhall Walk, London SE11 5HJ

2 4 6 8 10 9 7 5 3 1

© 2017 Jane Porter

The right of Jane Porter to be identified as author/illustrator of this work has been asserted by her in accordance with the Copyright, Designs and Patents Act 1988

This book has been typeset in Bembo

Printed in China

British Library Cataloguing in Publication Data: a catalogue record for this book is available from the British Library

ISBN 978-1-4063-6232-9

www.walker.co.uk

PINK LION

Jane Porter

WALKER BOOKS
AND SUBSIDIARIES

LONDON · BOSTON · SYDNEY · AUCKLAND

Arnold's life
was just right.

His family loved him.

They ate the nicest food.
And every day they
played games down
at the waterhole.

One day, a growling gang bounced by.
"It's a PINK lion!" they said.
"Living with a lot of BIRDS!"

"I'm a lion?" asked Arnold, puzzled.
"Yes, look at your face in the water,"
said one of the lions.

It was true, they did look alike.
They had the same curly hair and whiskers.
Could they really be related?
"Come along with us," said the
lions. "You should be out
roaring and hunting!"

Arnold thought perhaps he should give it a try.
"This is how we hunt," said the lions,
and off they raced.

Arnold wasn't sure he could run that fast.

"Next, some washing," said the lions.
"It's easy – just stick out your tongue
and lick!"

Arnold wasn't used to the furry taste, and wished he had his soap and sponge. Being a lion was very different from life at home.

RRROOOOOOOOOAR!

"Squork," said Arnold.

"I'm sorry," he said. "You've been very kind but I just can't do it. I'm not a proper lion. I think I'll go back to my family now."

Squork

But when he got home, something
terrible had happened.
A very nasty crocodile
had moved in.

"Excuse me," said Arnold, "this is our waterhole."
"Not any more," said the crocodile. "It's time
you and your feathery friends moved on.
I live here now."

Arnold didn't know what to say.

He looked at the sky.

He looked at the ground.

And then a strange feeling
like a hairy ball rose up
from deep inside
him ...

... and burst out of his mouth with a mighty

CRROOOOOO

The other lions heard Arnold calling.
Together they chased that crocodile
until he wished he had never
seen the waterhole.

ROOOOAR!

And Arnold's roar
was the **loudest** and
fiercest of all.

After that, life for Arnold went back to being just right again. And bath-time with his new cousins was more fun than ever.